The Art of Rejection

Because Dating's Not a Science—It's an Art

Hayley DiMarco
and Michael DiMarco

Revell
Grand Rapids, Michigan

Hungry Planet

© 2006 by Hungry Planet

Published by Fleming H. Revell
a division of Baker Publishing Group
P.O. Box 6287, Grand Rapids, MI 49516-6287
www.revellbooks.com

Printed in the United States of America

Library of Congress Cataloging-in-Publication Data
DiMarco, Hayley.
    The art of rejection / Hayley DiMarco and Michael
DiMarco.
        p.   cm.
    ISBN 10: 0-8007-3146-8 (pbk.)
    ISBN 978-0-8007-3146-5 (pbk.)
    1. Rejection (Psychology) 2. Interpersonal relations.
I. DiMarco, Michael. II. Title.
BF575.R35D56 2006
646.7'7—dc22   2006006875

Published in association with Yates & Yates, LLP, Literary Agents,
Orange, California.

Portions of this book have been adapted from material in *The
Dirt on Breaking Up* (Revell, 2004).

THE
MARRIABLE
GALLERY

# of Modern
Rejection
Art

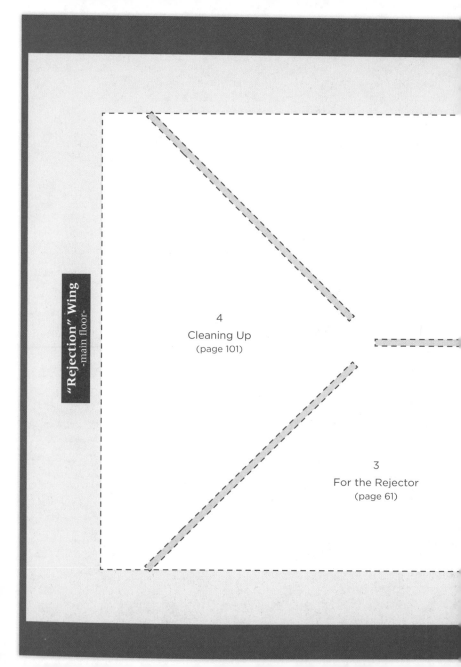

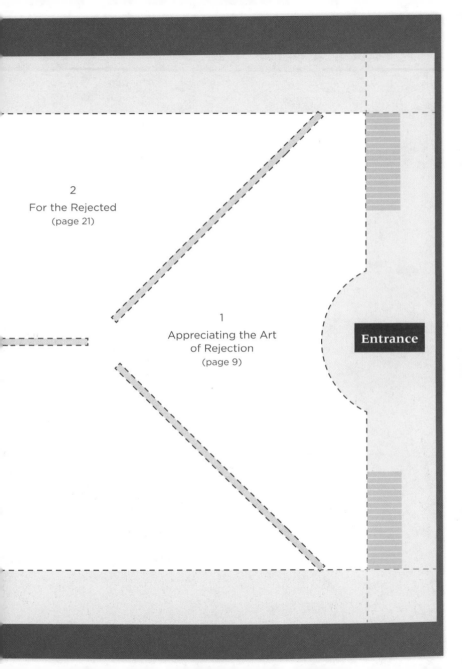

Entrance

Appreciating
the Art
of Rejection

1

Why Avoid the Unavoidable?

Time and time again, people try to avoid rejection in relationships either by not dating at all or by blurring the lines between friendship and dating. The irony is that rejection is a natural part of life. From our earliest days we remember picking teams in gym class, awkward middle school social events, the stress surrounding a potential prom date, and interviewing for our first job—all involving potential rejection. Even saying "I love you" to someone for the first time is fraught with rejection peril. Or is it?

Rejection is consistently portrayed as a negative. We hear the rejected say, "It feels like the end of the world" and "I never want to go through this again." We even said things strikingly similar in our not-too-distant pasts. The funny thing is that rejection always makes things better. You heard us: *rejection always makes things better.* If you truly believe that all things work together for good, then you have to believe that even rejection turns out for the good. That's why we see rejection as an art form instead of something that requires healing. Most of the time we hurt from rejection because we didn't have a proper perspective on the situation and we let things get out of control. Guess what? Rejection is your reset button.

"I don't think we should see each other anymore."

Click.

Reboot.

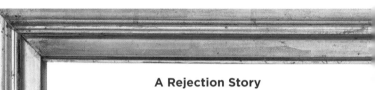

A Rejection Story

by Hayley

Back in college I was going out with this guy for maybe a couple months. I thought everything was just fine. One night we went out on this great date. Fine restaurant, great movie, good conversation. After a wonderful night he took me back to my apartment, walked in, sat down beside me on the couch, and said, "I don't think we should see each other anymore." Gulp! I didn't see that coming. Oh, the agony. I spent the next few weeks trying to get him to understand that I *was* someone that he *should* be dating.

Unfortunately, instead of grasping that the other person was doing us a favor by setting us free to find someone who was truly made for us, we lament over what we've "wasted": time, affection, gifts, and effort, among other wailings. We don't know if Thomas Edison was much of a ladies' man, but consider these quotes:

Genius is 1 percent inspiration
and 99 percent perspiration.

Be courageous, whatever setbacks America
has encountered, it has always emerged
as a stronger and more prosperous nation.

Results? Why, man, I have gotten lots of results!
If I find 10,000 ways something won't work,
I haven't failed.

Catch that? Edison understood that failure was only not trying. When the first 9,000 or so attempts to invent the lightbulb didn't work, he just considered himself *closer* to his goal. Edison clearly understood the Art of Rejection.

Look, maybe you've recently been dumped or had your ex freak out on you when you tried to break things off, and

12

as a result you're hurting. It was messy, and you don't want to repeat it. We've been there. We're still there! Not from dating (we don't swing) but in business, meeting new people at church, and returning clothes without a receipt, we still deal with rejection almost every day. But that's our point. You can't avoid the **R** word and still lead a full, colorful life.

Yes, this book will offer help to those of you still dealing with hurt. But our hope is that you'll come away from this little read with an authentic love of rejection! Our goal is to make you stop saying things like "I can't believe you're doing this to me!" and "Can't we give it just one more try?" and instead start saying confidently, "Well, I guess you weren't the one" and "Glad I found out now before we got married!"

Ahhhh, another rejection. I love brutal honesty.

Before we get started, let's do a little review. Life 101. There are only two outcomes for any relationship with a person of the opposite sex:

1. Marriage
2. Rejection

That's it! Since we only want you to get married once and there are going to be a lot of Mr. and Ms. Wrongs out there, let's learn the art of letting them down the right way and, as the case may sometimes be, accepting rejection ourselves. So sit back and learn from two people who have done it all wrong so you can do it right! Let's begin to appreciate the Art of Rejection.

Prelationship Rejection:
Why Guys Don't Ask

Before we get to dealing with the end of relationships, let's chat about the effect the *fear of rejection* can have on us way before the relationship even starts. If you read **Marriable**, you know all about our chapters entitled "Stand Up and Be a Man" and "Nice Guys Really Do Finish Last." The next page in our analysis of man-habits is his fear of rejection. This is the kind of fear that can hold a guy back from even asking a girl out on a date in the first place. As we see it, two types of fear keep guys from making a move: the fear of being rejected and the fear of rejecting others.

The fear of being rejected keeps scores of men on the dating sidelines, frustrating anxious and impatient women everywhere. Because of a guy's mythical mental belief that a girl saying "no thanks" will do irreparable harm to his psyche, nice guys are going dateless all across the land.

Paralyzed by fear, many times the nice guy will just opt to "settle" for the aggressive or persistent girl that asks *him* out, regardless of compatibility, because then he doesn't have to deal with the risk of rejection. But what happens is that the guy essentially becomes "trapped" in a badly matched relationship.

Double the trouble: When the fearful nice guy is combined with the "just friends" girl, the problem only doubles. He really likes her, and she's more than happy to hang out with him—she just doesn't like him "that way." Of course, because he never asks her out, he never gives her the opportunity to tell him he has no chance. So they have their own little "don't ask, don't tell" policy, all the while wasting time and stringing out emotions.

The first step in reducing the risk of rejection is learning how to flirt. Check out *The Art of the First Date* and *Marriable* for a crash course on doing the pre-dating dance.

The overarching answer to why guys should start risking rejection and start asking is in this taste from *Marriable*:

If you still are afraid of the chase, then consider this. What if we were to give you an endless supply of $1 bills with which you could buy lottery tickets at no risk to you? And say we guaranteed that in your lifetime, one of those dollars would hit the jackpot. Wouldn't you be laying those greenbacks down in a heartbeat, knowing your time was going to come? Trust us, we're not encouraging gambling or settling your retirement account with lotto tickets, but really, that's the type of control you have over your dating life. You have an endless supply of date invitations to offer—all you have to do is spend them. So get out there and start asking. It's the only manly thing to do.

Rejection is a part of life. When you live your life in fear of rejection, you look weak. And weakness isn't attractive. Learning the Art of Rejection is hot. It shows you're confident enough to ask for what you want, and you're not afraid of a little two-letter word.

Michael:

When I was in high school and college, I was half afraid of hearing the word "no" and half afraid of being seen as a player. So add those together and I was 115 percent <u>not</u> a fan of rejection. If I'd had the advice we're sharing in this book back then, maybe I would have gotten up the courage to talk to a cute girl or two at my restaurant job right out of high school.

Hayley:

A restaurant, by the way, that my mother and I used to eat at while you were employed there. But that's okay—we only missed fifteen years of not knowing each other and had to meet over the Internet while living two thousand miles apart.

Michael:

Well, I needed to do a lot of field research in order to write these books . . .

Hayley:

You mean <u>we</u> needed to. Let's not forget to remind readers that we did it all wrong so they don't have to!

17

If you thought fear of being rejected was weak, let us tell you about the "noble" men (and women!) who fear rejecting others. The fear of rejecting can be just as paralyzing as the fear of being rejected, but the one who fears rejecting gets to operate under the delusion that they are a noble soul. "I'm saving her feelings." "Women just fall too hard for me." "I don't want to be called a jerk when I don't like her like that." With so-called nice guys, sometimes this fear of rejecting is the real problem, but other times it's just an excuse masking a fear of rejection.

"Nice girls," on the other hand, tend to be oversensitive to the guy's feelings and think it's harmless to keep hanging out as "just friends" even though they know or suspect that he's interested in more (see "Can We Still Be Friends?" on page 102 for thoughts on the post-relationship issue).

Rejection is a fact of life. In fact, a healthy outlook on life means embracing rejection. No human always gets the job, gets the girl, or gets a large for the price of a medium. An older Garth Brooks song thanks God "for unanswered prayers." The lesson: rejection, even when we don't want or understand it, brings better things.

Girl Note: For all the guys out there who are afraid of "hurting" girls and so play it safe and don't ask anyone out, I say boo! I think I speak for most women when I say we'd rather have the chance to get hurt than never have a date at all. Staying home alone with a tub of ice cream is never our first option. Dating, risking, finding out if you could be the one is much more pleasurable. So save us your heroics and ask us out. Let us decide if we can handle the potential pain of unrequited love.

Hayley:

I have to confess that I have broken a heart or two with the "just friends" option. I thought for years that it was okay for me to spend a lot of time with a guy and become best buds, even though I knew he liked me more. I thought I was being nice, not hurting his feelings, by being friends even though I knew it would go nowhere. Knowing what I know now, I can say that it wasn't the kindest way to have treated them. It's better to pull the Band-Aid off fast than to let things drag on and let his feelings get too tied up in me.

Appreciating the Art of Rejection

This primate knows how to handle rejection. Or was it bananas?

Speaking of the job interview analogy, if a guy ever wants to do the hiring in life instead of just being hired (i.e., be the boss, be a leader), he's going to have to say "you're just not right for the job" to all the applicants who didn't get it. If a guy is afraid of rejecting people and can't handle their various reactions, he's probably not leadership material. At least not until he understands the Art of Rejection.

Because so many men are afraid to do the asking, more and more women are taking matters into their own hands and doing it themselves. All because men are too fearful of hearing the word *no* or too worried about not being the "hero." But this is a recipe for disaster. Women need to back off and be chaseable. That's how to land and keep a guy. Meanwhile, guys need to stand up and be men willing to risk for the chase. Believe us, she'll love you for it.

Now hurry up and ask that girl out so we can help you reject each other in the following pages!

For the Rejected

2

It Happens

People break up for lots of reasons. Sometimes these reasons seem valid, and sometimes they seem flat-out ridiculous. And when you are on the receiving end of the breakage, all reasons seem completely stupid. Either way, good reasons or not, you have to face the fact that it's happening. We aren't puppets. Dummies, maybe, but not puppets. We all have free will. That gift allows others to pick and choose who they spend their lives with. So breaking up becomes a natural and normal part of life, unless you are the one in millions who finds "the one" the first time you ever date. As for the rest of us, breakups will happen, and they can hurt.

Okay, back to our regularly scheduled rejection. Read on for some ways you can deal if you think you are about to be dumped.

Apocalypse Soon

Sure, it's warm and breezy outside your window, but the black storm clouds on the horizon and the Weather Channel tell you something's brewing. You can see the storm coming, so what do you do?

I love the smell of rejection in the morning.

Hold up. Before we start down into the basement with our canned goods, let's consider this: breakups rarely come out of nowhere. Even something as ever-changing as the weather has ten-day forecasts and StormTracker Doppler radar. There have been signs along the way. Of course, your favorite T-shirt might read "Ignorance is bliss," and you might have chosen to ignore the signs, but they *were* there. In fact, if you haven't heard the words of rejection yet but are wondering if they're coming your way, here are some signs you might not want to ignore.

23

8 Signs That Rejection Is Near

1. Their friends are acting strange. We tend to tell our friends what's going on in our love lives, so if his/her friends start to act weird, it might be a sign that something is up.
2. They don't want to talk as much anymore. On the phone they don't seem to want to talk as much as they used to. They cut the call short or don't seem to want to be on the phone with you.
3. Where's the love? All the nice mushy things they used to say are watered-down now. No more cards and cute notes. Suddenly "I love you" is replaced with "You're a great person" or "I don't deserve you." A change in communication might be a sign that rejection is on their mind.
4. PDA alert. Suddenly they won't hold your hand in public. No more arms around you or kisses in the mall. A halt to all public displays of affection is a surefire sign that something is amiss.

5. Name change. When suddenly you are no longer the boyfriend/girlfriend but are just intro'd as "my friend," you know what's up. In their mind you might have already become just a friend; you just haven't got the memo.
6. Fights. If you feel like you just can't seem to do anything without it erupting into major fightage, it's a sign that something is definitely wrong. Whether it's a sign of a coming breakup or of something worse, it's not a good thing.
7. Caught in the act. If you catch them in a lie about where they were, who they were with, or what they were doing and they weren't planning your surprise birthday party, then watch out. This isn't a good sign for the person's character or the relationship.
8. You can't do anything right. If it seems like everything you do is wrong, or "not how they would do it," or just plain stupid, then they could be letting you know that the end is near.

If you see one or more of these signs in your relationship, prepare to meet rejection with open arms. Preemptive strikes (breaking up with them first) are extreme. Just keep watch on your heart and start to prepare your graceful exit strategy. More on that later.

A Rejection Story
by Hayley

Talk about seeing the signs that a breakup is near. . . . I was with a guy once, and let's just say it was really serious. We were on the marriage path. He was a great guy, but something seemed wrong. He seemed to be getting shorter and shorter with me. I could sense his tension every time we were together. I soon figured out that he wanted out but wasn't going to do the breaking off because he was just too afraid to hurt me. One day after a long date, I turned to him in the car and said, "You don't love me." He kindly agreed, and so I said good-bye. And that was it. I drove off into the sunset, my heart in temporary pieces but my pride intact.

Now, you may already know the storm is coming or suspect it based on the list in this chapter. So what can you do? If you have some advance notice, you are in a great place—well, as great a place as you can be in right now. At least if you see it coming, you can do some advance prep.

Ask yourself a couple of questions. Well, don't just ask, answer them. These Q's will help you get your mind focused before your potential D-day (dump day).

1. Would you ever want to be with someone who doesn't want you?
2. If you could learn something through this, what would it be?
3. If God could speak to you through this, what is something that he would say?
4. What are five reasons this breakup will be good for you?

In the Moment:

What to Do (and Not Do) When It Happens to You

Now, before we get too far ahead into the getting-over-it zone, let's focus on that looming conversation and how to handle the actual moment of rejection.

5 Things You Can Do When Someone Is Rejecting You

1. Listen to their speech, tell them you are sorry to hear it but you understand, and then say good-bye.
2. Tell them that you are glad that they told you their feelings and you completely understand that they have to go with their gut.
3. If the only thing you want to say is going to be mean, keep your mouth shut (literally). Then nod your head, turn around, and walk out.
4. Tell them that it has been nice getting to know them, wish them luck in their search, and then turn around and leave.
5. Let them know that because of how you feel for them, you can't continue to be friends, and it would be best for you to just go your separate ways and remember each other well.

28

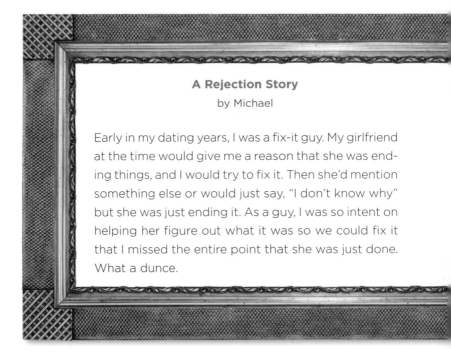

A Rejection Story

by Michael

Early in my dating years, I was a fix-it guy. My girlfriend at the time would give me a reason that she was ending things, and I would try to fix it. Then she'd mention something else or would just say, "I don't know why" but she was just ending it. As a guy, I was so intent on helping her figure out what it was so we could fix it that I missed the entire point that she was just done. What a dunce.

Share your rejection stories at
www.marriable.com

If these responses to a major heartbreak seem very short and unemotional, *it's because they are.* Now listen, if you have been going out with the person for two years and a lot has been going on between you, then you might need to talk it through. But if it hasn't been eons together, keep this breakup short and to the point. Showing emotion is okay, but breaking down and having a soon-to-be embarrassing moment will not help you at all. And it certainly won't help them. We know that their feelings aren't your major concern right now, but think about it. You care about this person, so keep the faith, treat them how you would want to be treated, and let them have their feelings and their choices. Remember, they just released you to go find your soul mate (or something like it). Get out, go home, call your best bud, and debrief. Talk through what you will look for in your next attempt at inventing the lightbulb. Don't be surprised if it takes more than one rejection to cement this new positive appreciation for the Art of Rejection. You might have a ton of muscle memory built up. If you feel like crying, cry into your pillow or on a friend's shoulder, or go play hoops—do whatever it takes to avoid showing your newly minted ex your pain.

In case you are still not sure about this rejected thing, here are 10 Things Not to Do When Being Rejected

1. Don't ask them what you did wrong. Anything they say here will discourage you more. So don't go there.

2. Don't beg them to change their mind, *because they just might.* Then you are stuck in a severely dysfunctional relationship. Congratulations! You convinced someone who doesn't want you that they should hang around and delay you from meeting someone better!

3. Don't argue with their decision. It will only make you feel more rejected when they stick to it and will make the whole thing much more of a trauma (rhymes with drama!).

4. Don't yell at them. Lashing out and trying to destroy them is not the best option. It won't make you feel better, and it will make you look desperate.

5. Don't cry like a baby. You might not have the Art of Rejection down quite yet, so showing emotion is normal. But fight off the sobbing until you get out of there.

6. Don't promise to get revenge on them. This is a desperate attempt at manipulation. See #2 above.

7. Don't remind them of all the good times you've had together. All this will do is make you feel worse because you will be remembering all the good times that are ending.

8. Don't tell them the list of what you think is wrong with them. This isn't a slamfest. No matter how much you think it will help, when you leave, you will still feel just as empty.

9. Don't run out and tell everyone what a jerk they are. That will only make you look like the desperate jilted one. Handle yourself with grace, be cool, be calm, and have an appreciation for your freedom to find "the one." You'll look like even more of a catch.

10. Don't act like they have destroyed you, because they haven't. They haven't even hurt you. We know, that doesn't seem true, but the pain is there because your expectations did not match up with reality. The only way you will be destroyed is if you let yourself be destroyed. It isn't what happens to you in life but what you think about it and how you react to it that matters.

8 Reasons They Might Give When Rejecting You

1. "I just need space"

This one is interesting. Sometimes when people break up, they say they just need some space. Half the time it is just a way of saying, "I don't want to date you anymore," but the other half of the time it means, "I feel smothered by you." Here's the interesting if not tragic common response of the rejected: they want to vigorously defend themselves as a non-smotherer. Guess what? If you do this, you're proving their point. You're smothering them while being rejected!

Sometimes when someone says they need space, all they really need is space. So give it to them. Their sense of your neediness might fall away, and they might return to you. But don't bet on it. They could just repeat the cycle because they have a low tolerance for, well, you. Go find a match who can't imagine life without you.

2. "I want to date someone else"

This rejection line goes straight for your ego and tests your confidence. At least with the "I just need space" rejection, they're going to be alone for a while too. But this one means you're the only one flying solo—you and millions of other people, of course. (Don't you hate those injections of perspective at a time like this?) The trap in this rejection is when you start to compare yourself with your newly anointed replacement. **Bad idea**. The bottom line is that they don't want to date you, and that means they will date others. So really, in any breakup, they are wanting to date other people. This rejection just means they're ready to start that evening. You have no choice with this one. Don't try to compete with the other person or plead your case. Don't get angry with the other person; it isn't their fault. It was the choice of your boyfriend/girlfriend, and that choice was theirs to make. So lay off, lie low, and be thankful their new crush came along now instead of two years from now.

3. "It's not you, it's me"

The truth is, it's **not** you, it **is** them. Their decision to reject you has to do with what **they** want. With this approach, what they are really saying is they can't put their finger on why they're rejecting you, but they just aren't feeling it. Or they have reasons that would sound frivolous, shallow, or lame, and they don't want to have to defend them. Congratulations—you just avoided being stuck with someone potentially frivolous, shallow, and lame!

4. "I need to concentrate on my (fill in the blank)"

Schooling, career, faith, sick family member, fill in the blank. This is actually a very mature reason to call it quits. They are being honest with you and telling you that they can't handle the pressures of their personal or professional commitments and a relationship at the same time. In other words, they have enough maturity to say, "I'm not mature enough to juggle everything, like, say, someone who's married would." Bravo for them. Of course, this reason, like any other method of rejection, can just be used to let you down easy, so don't hang onto any hopes of things picking back up. Make this a clean break and expect them to have to do a lot of work to get you back.

A Rejection Story
by Hayley

Ugh. I think the "I need to concentrate on my (blank)" breakup was one of the most painful I've ever experienced. It felt to me like his "blank" was another woman. I mean, why couldn't I compete with his "blank"? After that one I really messed up. I tried to apologize for whatever *I* had done to bring this on. The "blank" couldn't really be the reason, I thought. But after a few attempts to prove to him that I was his dream girl, I finally gave up, and soon after that I met the *real* man of my dreams. And all my experiences with rejection really did lead to something better.

5. "I just don't want to see you anymore"

We know you want to know why. You want a better reason than this. You want reasons, dates, episodes, flaws, all the details, but sometimes there isn't any one thing they can (or want to) point to. They just don't want to see you anymore. They might be bored, they might just be ready for something new, but whatever it is, you don't have a right to know. So don't ask. Think Edison and chalk it up as another way not to make a lightbulb.

6. "I just don't trust you anymore"

Sounds like there's a backstory to this one that you know all about. Trust takes time to build, and if you did something to break their trust, it will take time to get it back. Arguing about it with them won't help. Tell them you are sorry, and then let them move on. That is the most gracious way to handle this one.

7. "I just don't love you anymore"

How could they? How could someone just stop loving you? We know, it seems impossible, but the truth is that the feeling they *thought* was love doesn't feel good anymore, and so they've decided they are out of love. Learn from this: You don't want anyone who loves solely based on a feeling. Love is dedicated in good times and bad. Remember, dating is to help you find out if you can continue to love someone during the times when feelings of infatuation disappear. If you are dating someone who only loves you when it feels good, then they don't love you.

37

8. "This relationship is just too much pressure for me"

That's too bad, really, because a relationship shouldn't be a pressure, it should be a pressure reliever. Maybe you put too much pressure on them to be what you wanted them to be. Try to loosen up next time. Or maybe they just put too much pressure on themselves, in which case they need to loosen up. Some people are afraid of commitment, while others push for too much too soon. Use this as an opportunity to self-examine to see if a relationship with you is closer to pressure-free or pressure-filled. Either way, let them be free. Don't pressure them more by demanding that they work it out. Too much pressure!

There they are. Stand back and admire the awesome wonder of rejection. So many ways that people can set you free to find true love! When you look at that person rejecting you over coffee, just remember Edison and say to yourself, "I gotta find me a lightbulb."

Let's Just Be Friends:

| Why You Should Beware of Partial Rejection |

In most cases, when a couple breaks up, one person isn't rejecting the other as a human being, only as a potential mate. Common interests remain, and even common attraction, but without the expectations and pressure. That's why sometimes after the breakup the relationship seems to get better. It's more fun. The other person becomes more attentive and even more affectionate. It will make you question whether you should stay with it since it seems so good. This is a lie! The relationship is not better. So what's really happening here?

- Maybe they are trying to soften the blow of the breakup and they think this helps.
- Maybe they feel free to be more attentive now that the pressure of the relationship is off.
- Maybe they can't be alone and subconsciously will be super nice until they secure a relationship with someone else.

No matter why this phenomenon happens, the other person probably doesn't even know they are doing it and wouldn't admit it if they did. So this is where you have to take a stand and remember that this new friendship phase of the relationship is not a waiting room for wedded bliss. The rejector is going to find someone soon enough, and you'll be left to deal with a second rejection from the same person. Don't sit by like a dog looking for table scraps. Let the relationship be over.

The Prostitution of Being "Just Friends"

Okay, make sure you're sitting down for this part, because it might throw you for a loop. We've said in *Marriable* that being just friends is a waste of time, but for you special readers of *The Art of Rejection* here's a new one for you. If you're still "hanging out" with someone who no longer wants to date you, you are prostituting yourself. Think about it, a prostitute trades one "hard to get" element of a relationship in exchange for something else, and it just so happens that most prostitutes exchange sex for money. When you decide to go the "just friends" route with someone who has already rejected you, you're engaged in platonic prostitution. That's right, you heard us. You're sharing everything but the physical, feelings, and your future. You're sharing coffee, companionship, your hopes and dreams. Renting movies, going to the park. Everything a real relationship has, except for physical chemistry, commitment, and a future together. Oh, sure, *one* of you has the chemistry, but the other one doesn't. In platonic prostitution what you're trading is "friendship" in order to get the time and attention of someone who is no longer attracted to you. And ultimately what they are paying you is a dash of hope, your hope that one day they'll change their minds and realize that they really love you. Though they emphatically deny there is *any* hope of rekindling your relationship, you have to admit that there is a smidgen of hope in your heart that they just might come around.

What most often happens is that your ex makes it perfectly clear that they no longer want to date you, and they think therefore that they are off the hook with you emotionally. Now they are free and clear to spend all the time in the world with you without feeling like they are leading you on. After all, they *told* you there was no chance for you, so any feelings you have for them now must be purely platonic, like theirs are. They lie to you and to themselves that you can be just friends without feeling any of the chemistry that you used to feel for them. And therefore you won't end up being hurt by them when they finally find someone they *do* want to date and no longer have time for you.

41

Sure you won't.

It's like this, right now you are the stand-in, the stunt double if you will, for their future soul mate. And once they find that soul mate, you can't come crying to them about "how could they!" because they told you all along that this relationship wasn't going anywhere. It's ingenious really—they have a temporary "partner" without any of the pressure. No more evenings alone, no more rejection from people they could be casually dating until they find their dream person. You are their one stop shop for companionship—for now.

Even if you aren't spending all of your time together, if you are continuing some kind of friendship, they are still using you. If you are available when they call, hanging out with them at all, or even just there as a listening ear when they need you, you're cheating yourself out of a real relationship.

The best thing to do in these situations is to refuse the friendship. You aren't being unfair or vindictive by denying that relationship. And we're not saying "don't be friendly." What you should be doing is being more realistic and refusing to be used. People can't have all the benefits of dating without the commitment of a dating relationship. And we aren't talking about any kind of commitment more than one that says "yes, I'm interested, and yes, there's hope." This isn't that tall of an order. So don't buy the lie that being "just friends" is beneficial or even helpful no matter what they might say.

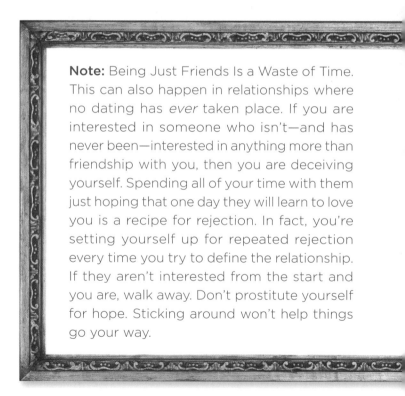

Note: Being Just Friends Is a Waste of Time. This can also happen in relationships where no dating has *ever* taken place. If you are interested in someone who isn't—and has never been—interested in anything more than friendship with you, then you are deceiving yourself. Spending all of your time with them just hoping that one day they will learn to love you is a recipe for rejection. In fact, you're setting yourself up for repeated rejection every time you try to define the relationship. If they aren't interested from the start and you are, walk away. Don't prostitute yourself for hope. Sticking around won't help things go your way.

Things you can do instead of hanging out with someone who _doesn't_ "like you, like you."

- Wash your hair
- Hang out with someone with matching chromosomes
- Take a class
- Learn to cook
- Buy a pottery wheel
- Take up archery
- Climb a mountain
- Read a book
- Do your laundry
- Pray for world peace
- Eat a sandwich

Art Appraisal Time

You've read a little about how we want you to embrace the Art of Rejection as a sign of better things to come. But old feelings are hard to shake. You are going to feel like you've been rejected because, well, you have. And up till now you've probably had a negative view of rejection or been programmed by all your lovesick fool friends. But the reality is, your ex isn't the source of that hurt you're feeling. The thing that makes all of this so gnarly and tough to spin positively is that your dreamworld has been shaken—all those white picket fences of the future that surrounded the two of you were just turned into splinters by a trac-

44

tor-trailer rig hauling pallets and pallets of rejection. And your new ex was at the wheel, crushing your dreams of the future. Those dreams could really be fulfilled by anyone, but you had pegged Mad Max (or Maxine) as your hope, your hero.

A Rejection Story
by Michael

Seems like so long ago, but the worst way I ever handled rejection was trying to guilt the other person into giving it another shot. It was so manipulative. They say desperate times call for desperate measures. But take it from me, there's nothing redeeming about desperate love. It does irrational things, even destructive things. If you start doing or saying things you normally wouldn't, like doing the fetal position rock or telling them you can't live without them, hit your reset button with a sledgehammer. Sure, your dignity comes back, but it's pretty embarrassing to beg someone to love you.

It's normal for dreams to take wing. Pigs, not so much.

This is what's key for "next time": keeping perspective, guarding your heart, and knowing the odds. It's normal to let your dreams take wing. But it's also normal for rejection to hurt like heck when you do. That's why we have to learn the Art of Rejection—how to handle both ends with hope and a positive outlook.

Now you have to adapt and overcome Mr. or Ms. "Rejection Is My Co-Pilot" not being in your life anymore. And that can be tough since you're used to having them around. Even with a positive appreciation of rejection, you're still going to go through some life changes in your daily routine. So now it's time to take some action to get your life back on track. It's time to get down to the getting over it and regaining perspective.

Your first assignment is to study what love really is. Check out one of the oldest and best definitions of love from that best-selling book the Bible. In fact, this passage is probably read at more weddings than any other:

Love is patient and kind; love does not envy or boast; it is not arrogant or rude. It does not insist on its own way; it is not irritable or resentful; it does not rejoice at wrongdoing, but rejoices with the truth. Love bears all things, believes all things, hopes all things, endures all things.

1 Corinthians 13:4–7

This is actually a perfect synopsis of how you should conduct yourself when being rejected. You are patient and kind. You're not envious of the next crush they have. You check your arrogance at the door and leave rudeness in the dust in exchange for grace under pressure. You're not celebrating revenge or them "getting what they deserve." This definition of love actually endorses falling in love with the Art of Rejection. Because when someone rejects you, you can "rejoice in the truth" that this wasn't the person for you and that person is still to come.

47

A Quiz

Rejection Rookie or Pro?

How well are you handling rejection?

1. When my girlfriend/boyfriend told me they wanted to break up, I:
   a. asked them why
   b. begged them to give me a second chance
   c. told them I understood and left it at that
2. The day after the breakup, I:
   a. called my ex to see if they changed their mind
   b. cleaned my place top to bottom
   c. called friends to see if they knew anything about it and could help get us back together
   d. thought of ways to get revenge
3. Right now I:
   a. hate them for what they did
   b. am really bummed, but I have to let them go
   c. am working on ways to get them back
4. When I think about six months from now, I think of:
   a. being back with him/her
   b. being over this yucky feeling
   c. still being miserable without him/her
5. Although it doesn't feel like it right now, I know that this will get better.   True   False

1. a = 2, b = 3, c = 1
2. a = 3, b = 1, c = 3, d = 3
3. a = 3, b = 1, c = 3
4. a = 2, b = 1, c = 3
5. T = 1, F = 3

5–7: Masterpiece in the making. It looks like you've got a healthy perspective and you're making the transition all right. You're not worrying about whether it was your fault or the other person's fault. Rejection's just a fact of life. You thought they were a match, and you were right, but you're looking for a lightbulb!

8–15: Heartache. The pain is overwhelming right now, but we promise, it will get better. Try to remember that most of the junk you're feeling is mourning your lost hopes and dreams, not the actual person. Those are things that you can control and that any person you meet tomorrow could potentially fulfill. Keep your focus on good things in your life like your faith, your family, and your friends (go easy on the other *f*, food), and don't let your brain wander off and confuse the truth with fiction.

49

Rejection Restoration

Remember that positive results always spring from rejection, even though you might not feel too positive right now. Here are some ways to find hope and promise out of what you used to call hurt.

What's done is done. There's no such thing as partial rejection or a partial breakup. Whenever you see your ex or something reminds you of them, slam the door on any possibility that they're the one. Say, "I don't know what we had, but it sure wasn't a lightbulb!"

Forget about what others think. Similar to the guy who won't ask a girl out for fear of rejecting her down the line and her thinking (or saying) he's a jerk, being afraid of other people's opinions of us is a waste of time. Soon enough you're going to be dating and even marrying the person of your dreams, and your friends will say, "Boy, they're the happiest I've ever seen them!" (Not that you care . . .)

Find one trusted friend. You need one person who won't take sides and help you place blame in the situation but instead is a positive influence in helping you move on, appreciating the rejection along the way.

Create your own propaganda campaign. Start a journal emphasizing your positive perspective on what this breakup means. Write down how things are going to be different and better. Don't give yourself permission to wallow in negativity in print. By all means, cry out for help and strength in the situation, but don't let anger, bitterness, or resentment drip from your pen. Sure, it might feel cathartic, but unless you're truly writing it down to release it and never revisit it, it can be just as destructive as walking around thinking negative thoughts.

I like a good run after each rejection.

Just do it. Get out and do the things that make you happy. Physical things are best for releasing endorphins, but hobbies, arts, and home projects release the steam and give you a feeling of accomplishment as well.

File a written autopsy. Record everything about the relationship from the time of its death to its cause of death. Natural causes, blunt force trauma to the ego, whatever. If someone dies of organ failure (heart, anyone?), genetic and environmental conditions may have contributed. Write down the symptoms, conversations,

51

and events that lead to the ultimate demise of "us" and research how diseases like yours and theirs can be treated or avoided for your future health. This shouldn't be a whine fest where you overanalyze all the heartache you experienced at their hands. It's a chance for you to examine your actions and make sure you aren't doing something destructive that can be avoided in the future. And to remind yourself that this wasn't the relationship for you. When you are done with this process, file your autopsy report where you can access it when you start questioning if the relationship is really dead.

A silly hind sighting.

Hindsight is dumb. Yes, it's usually accurate, but revisiting the past is about as useful as worrying about what others think. In other words, it's a complete waste of time. History is useful for studying so it's not repeated, but not for some sick emotional obstacle course. When you start pining for the person who rejected you, it's time to reread the autopsy. If the past had been different, you just would have been with someone you weren't meant to be with for longer than you were. So let go of the shoulda's and woulda-been's and move on.

Plan for future success. This is a result of a well thought-out autopsy. Make a plan and mental regimen for success in your next relationship. Make sure you've identified what you did wrong in the last one and how you want to act and feel differently in the next. Besides reviewing your written autopsy occasionally, your mental regimen can include repeating strategic phrases to yourself over and over. For example, if your last three crushes have said, "I need more space," choose a phrase to repeat that will keep you from being a clingy guy (e.g., "chicks dig mystery" or "remember to have a life"). If guys keep saying, "I like you as a friend," say to yourself, "I'm worth pursuing" or "I won't be his future girlfriend's stand-in." Be sure to review your plan for success often and make sure that it's laced with the perspective that rejection is normal and to be expected more often than not.

Don't repeat rejection rituals. Avoid any past habits of forced solitude or reckless social behavior in response to rejection. Temper your negative muscle memory with activities that accomplish the exact opposite goal. If you normally would pour yourself into work to drown your brain in details, go for long, silent walks during your lunch break. If your typical response is to start throwing parties, try working on projects in solitude. Likewise, if you tend to put your hermit hat on, get out and socialize with your same-sex friends. As Mr. Miyagi once said, balance is key, Daniel-san.

Be a good Samaritan. When we're feeling our lowest, helping others actually makes us feel better about our world because it reminds us that the world isn't all about us. Volunteer with strangers or attend to those family members or long lost friends you've neglected during your adventures in romance gone wrong.

Hang up your spurs for a while. Some people avoid dealing with rejection by covering it up with a new relationship or at least "getting back on the horse." Whoa, cowpoke! You need time to assess why you got bucked in the first place, to analyze your taste in horses, and to confirm you were facing the right way before you start riding the range again.

> It's not what happens to you
> but what you *think* about
> what happens to you that
> affects your emotions.

A Better Understanding of the Art

If you can control your mind, you can control your feelings. Even researchers have proof to back up that truth. That means you don't have to be tortured by pain and agony like you might think. We know a really cool little trick that will make stuff like this breakup a lot easier to live through. But like anything good, it takes work. So you have two choices right now:

1. You can stay miserable and pray that someday it will just wear off by itself.
2. You can try something new and see if your whole life doesn't do a major flip-flop.

If you are up for the flip-flop challenge, here goes: It's not **what happens to you** but what you **think about what happens to you** that affects your emotions.

55

It's like this: Let's say there are two people; we'll call them Sal and Hal. They are both in an avalanche and end up with really bad frostbite, broken bones, and horrible headaches. Sal whines about this horrible avalanche that messed up his life. I mean, heck, he lost a toe to frostbite, what could be worse? His life is miserable, and he's totally depressed because his little piggy went sledding.

Now Hal, who lived through the same trauma, feels way different. He's okay with life. He thinks everything happens for a reason and so there must be something cool about this avalanche. I mean, he *did* get interviewed by every news show, including ***Good Morning America***. He might even get to write a book about the whole thing. Sure, he lost a toe and broke some bones. He'll be in the hospital for at least another month. But he's whistling instead of whining. He's happy instead of sad.

So what's up with the avalanche? How come one guy says it has filled him with wonder and the other guy is miserable? Well, it sure isn't because the avalanche has all this power over people's emotions. Only people have power over their emotions, not a bunch of white powder. It's all about choices. Avalanche happens, as they say; now choices have to be made. Are you gonna whine about it or smile about it? You can't fix it, change it, or redo it. You can't analyze it to change the way it turned out. You can't do anything but decide how you are going to feel about it.

Freaky thing, but you can look at any catastrophe anywhere in the world and find two people who feel completely opposite about the whole thing. And it's all because of how they think about the situation. One says, "Whose fault is this?" and starts pointing fingers. The other asks, "What can I do to help?" It's called personal accountability. Change your way of thinking, and you change your way of feeling. It's that simple.

John Miller has written two excellent books on personal accountability: QBQ: The Question Behind the Question and Flipping the Switch: Unleash the Power of Personal Accountability Using the QBQ.

Control my mind? I hope that doesn't require *another* remote.

Sounds easy enough, but how are you possibly going to learn how to control your mind long enough to control your emotions? You probably can't even concentrate long enough to read a restaurant menu right now, so how can you focus your mind to beat your emotions?

It's like a DVD—your mind, that is. It keeps playing these old movies over and over. Stuff from the past, stuff about that terrible night, that awful set of events. Bad stuff, good stuff, freaky stuff, stuff that makes you worry and cry and freak. And each day you play this DVD over and over in your mind, so your mind thinks that's just the way it is.

But your mind isn't as all-powerful and as in control of you as you think it is. It's actually more like an animal: It only believes what you show it and let it daydream about. In fact, it is so gullible that it can be tricked and even retrained like a dog.

Try this trick (no, not play dead). Whenever you feel a negative or hurtful thought about your breakup enter your head, replace it with something positive about your life and future that the breakup fixed. Whatever you think about over and over becomes a permanent video in your head and affects what you do. That's why keeping your mind on higher, more positive things keeps us so stable and healthy. Then watch that old so-called horrible day become less and less hurtful and more and more part of giving you a new lease on life. Ah, to appreciate rejection!

Appreciate rejection yet?
Tell us about it at www.marriable.com

For the
Rejector

3

Should I Stay or Should I Go?

First off, let us commend you for being the rejector. Although it sounds odd, we say congratulations for realizing that a new chapter in your life is about to be written and another chance at inventing the lightbulb is about to be had! Far too often people stay in a relationship too long when they know that it should be over.

We've both done such a thing to famous proportions—let things drag on and on when we knew we didn't want to be with the other person. Why do this when it was just wasting our time and the other person's time?

Most of us are programmed to think that everything involving breakups or rejection is negative. For some odd reason, in things besides relationships we can say "God has a plan" and "all things work together for good," but in our relationships and in dealing with rejection, we seem to throw all that out the window. It's all because we lose perspective. But what was lost now is found! So let's look at why and how to reject someone the right way.

A Reason Is a Reason Is a Reason

People tell us one of the major reasons they're spending a lot of time thinking about a breakup before the actual breakup is that they are trying to figure out how to defend their reasons to the rejected. So let's see if we can help speed up the process by looking at two major categories of reasons for calling it quits: little things and deal breakers.

Here are some examples of what could fall into each of these categories:

Little Things
- body odor
- sound of their laugh
- eating habits
- nervous ticks
- their relationship with their mother
- Diet Coke over Diet Pepsi

Deal Breakers
- wanting kids versus not wanting kids
- where they want to ultimately live
- lifestyle and financial status

- faith
- lack of chemistry
- no evidence of love—includes things like abuse, lies, and destructiveness

Some of you might be thinking, "Oh, great, I've got to come up with a deal breaker." Wrong. There is no unspoken rule that says you can't break up over one little thing. As hard as it might be for the rejected to fathom it, body odor, the sound of their laugh, or any other one little thing is enough to pull the plug if you say so.

You don't really have to have a reason other than that you just don't feel like dating them anymore. It's your life, your choice. Even though any reason is a good enough reason, we'll still take you through some more definite deal breakers and tell you how to deliver your big bombshell while doing the least amount of damage. If you want to see some examples of why others break up, check out this list:

Abuse—This one seems like a no-brainer, but for some reason it isn't. You think that it's your fault, and you want to fix it. You think that things will get better if you just **do better.** But that isn't true. Abuse is never okay. Never, never, no matter what you've done, it's *never* okay. So if you are in a relationship that is abusive physically or emotionally, you are in the wrong relationship. Get out now!

Destruction—Two people can destroy each other in ways other than abuse. If you find that your spirit is weakening, your heart is breaking, and you don't know why, then maybe you are in a destructive relationship. If you can't say that this person makes you better emotionally, mentally, and spiritually, you need to think about changing the situation. Relationships should make you both better, not worse.

Lies—It's a sad truth, but after one of you has been caught in a lie, it's very hard to win back the trust of the other. That's why lies are so horrific; they tear away at the foundation of the relationship and mess it up, usually permanently. If you've been lied to, we guarantee you that it will take a lot of time and effort on the other person's part to ever get you to trust them again. This isn't a healthy relationship. If you can't trust the other person, then you shouldn't be dating them, period.

65

Cheating—Don't give in on this one. If you've both decided together that you're going to be exclusive and your "someone" is willing to cheat on you, you can't trust them. They have destroyed that. It's just a sign of bad character. Better to find out now than after you're married. If someone is willing to tell you that you are the only one and then go out with someone behind your back, they don't have the kind of character that is worthy of you. And remember, it is your soon-to-be ex's fault, not the fault of the person they hooked up with.

Fights—Fights are normal. When two people spend a lot of time together, they are bound to argue, and that's okay. But if fighting is a daily occurrence, this isn't a good fit. This relationship should be the most comfortable and safe relationship you have. Fights bad, getting along good.

Boredom—Be careful with this one. Boredom is a part of life, and it might be partially your fault that you are bored. But if it's obvious that there is no hope for your boredom, then walk. Don't hang on because you're hoping for some magical improvement. Boredom isn't a good sign for the future, so break it off while the breaking is easier than it will be later down the road.

Distance—If one of you is moving, it is only natural to start to think about a breakup. Dating over long distances is tough, and if you just aren't up for the loneliness, maybe breaking up is what you need to do.

Trusted objection—This one is tough, but if your parents or best friends object to your boyfriend/girlfriend, it's not a good sign. As much as you hate to admit it, these people probably know you better than anyone. Remember, wise people seek counsel in their lives. It's smart and healthy to get the advice of the people who know you best as you drive down the bumpy road of life.

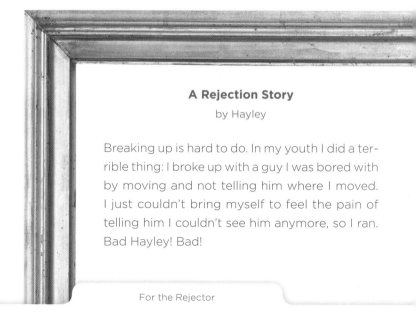

A Rejection Story
by Hayley

Breaking up is hard to do. In my youth I did a terrible thing: I broke up with a guy I was bored with by moving and not telling him where I moved. I just couldn't bring myself to feel the pain of telling him I couldn't see him anymore, so I ran. Bad Hayley! Bad!

For the Rejector

Even with an appreciation for the Art of Rejection, it's still hard. People who are in an unhealthy relationship find it really hard to leave, even though most people would think it would be the most obvious and easy thing for them to do. But making the decision to reject someone by leaving them is always difficult, no matter who they are or what the circumstances.

If you have a sense that you want out of the relationship, go with that. Don't be afraid of hurting the other person's feelings, because you aren't in control of how they will react. You are only in control of your own life. In the end, breaking it off at the first sign of serious trouble will be much better than letting it linger until it becomes more and more painful to break up.

Location, Location, Location

Thinking about a few things first will help you get going in this process. First, since you know it's going to be hard for both of you, don't have the "rejection" talk in the middle of a busy restaurant (sorry, Hollywood) or in front of your roommate who's watching TV. Find a less public place where you can both be as comfortable as possible.

Rejection Review

Acceptable reasons to break up:
- You don't like being with them anymore
- One of you is relocating
- Your feelings have changed
- They lied to you, cheated on you, or did something to you that you can't get over
- They have plans for the future that conflict with yours
- They like Diet Coke

You can't just say, "I've decided I just don't like you anymore—see ya!" and run out the door. You've got to offer closure in direct proportion to the length and commitment of the relationship. If you've only been dating a while and things aren't that serious, then the breakup can be short and sweet. But if you've been together for two years and have talked about marriage, then the breakup requires sensitivity and more explanation. For those of you who've never had closure and are closure-clueless, that means taking the time and care to end it and, watch this now, don't miss this point . . . ending it! Tell them about your decision and realize that it's not your job to make them feel better. This probably used to be your job, but you're resigning from your position. There's no two weeks' notice given. Heck, you've probably been giving signs this was going to happen for longer than two weeks.

Now, even though it's not your job to make them feel better, you still need to listen to them and their feelings, again, in direct proportion to the length and degree of commitment of the relationship. This isn't easy or fun, but you have to give the person a break and let them vent a little (hopefully they've read this book too and won't create too much drama). It's all part of the deal.

Now let's get to the details. We'll start with the easy stuff—what *not* to do if you've been dating for a while. Here we go . . .

You've got to offer closure in direct proportion to the length and commitment of the relationship.

How *Not* to Break Up

Don't break up:
- in a note
- over the phone
- by telling a friend to tell them for you
- in an IM or email
- before a party you're going to together
- in front of other people
- on their birthday or any other major holiday
- on national TV (a la *Jerry Springer*)
- by making them so mad *they* break up with *you*
- by moving and not telling them where you moved

If you've had any sort of ongoing, committed relationship with this person, you are not allowed to use any electronic device in order to break up with them, except in extraordinary circumstances like a long distance relationship where you would have to hop on a plane to get there.

If you've only been out on a few dates and you'll probably rarely if ever see this person again, using a phone is acceptable. If you met online and with the exception of one or two dates the bulk of your correspondence was via email, it's now acceptable etiquette to break things off with the "Send" button.

Primarily speaking to the ladies, as with anything, safety first. If you think a guy's going to go nutso on you, do the rejecting over the phone, in public, or by email, whichever you're more comfortable with. Again, these are extraordinary circumstances.

One thing you're going to hear over and over from us regarding the Art of Rejection is the phrase "in direct proportion to the length and commitment of the relationship." Always consider this when choosing your method and location. It'll make things a little easier when the time comes.

Note to wimpy rejectors: If you know you're terrible at cutting things off clean and always cave when in person, abandon all the rules on method and location and break things off over the phone. If you're a tele-wimp as well, use email. It's better to deliver full rejection from a distance than partial rejection in person.

The Law of Polarized Sensitivity: Girls want to talk it out, guys want to fix it. So girls, don't beat around the bush by using too many words. And guys, don't soften the blow by offering up scenarios that you're not interested in just to make her feel better.

La Rejectorita

Okay, girls, we hate to say it, but guys are kinda slow. They need lots of explaining. And being hunters and creatures who love a challenge, they will look for every possible angle to keep you once you decide it's over. Your rejecting them is just a harder level in the video game of life—nothing they can't conquer, they think. So for a girl breaking up with a guy, it is crucial that you don't hint around about things but be totally direct. If you hint, he'll never get a clue. It's like when the guy in *Dumb and Dumber* asked the girl, "So what are my chances?" and she said, "One in a million." He smiled and shouted, "So you're telling me there's a chance!" Hey, you have to tell him point blank that you don't want to date him anymore.

Girls love to talk things out. It's just girl nature. But for guys, a talk is an opportunity to try to "fix" things. Some guys will use "the talk" as an opportunity to try to get you back, so letting them go on and on really defeats the purpose. It gives them hope, and that's incompatible with you wanting freedom. Giving them hope is like lying to them. In the long run they will be better off if they can just move on and get over you rather than hanging onto some morbid hope that they will get you back.

74

Helping a guy explore his feelings and share them with you while you're breaking up with him makes no sense at all. But because you girls love to understand why he's reacting the way he is, here are a few of the biggies so you don't have to ask him and you can protect the completeness of the rejection.

Mr. Short and Sweet

Girls, realize that guys are not big "feelings" talkers. Even though you are the one breaking up, you may still want to talk things through with him. But he may not. He may just say, "Okay, if that's what you want," and turn around and walk. If he does this, girls, do not go after him and try to get him to talk about what he *feels* about all of this. Most guys will need time to go away and figure it out on their own. To drag out the feelings talk can be just plain selfish if he's one of these kind of guys.

He's short but been known to crumble.

Mr. Emotionless

If he just sits there emotionless, you are going to feel like the whole relationship was a lie. You think that if you really meant something to him, he should show some sort of emotion. Anything! If he doesn't, don't let yourself get caught in the trap of thinking he never really liked you anyway. That will destroy you. Just let him go and stick with your plan.

Dr. Weepy, Mr. Angry

Much like the Jekyll/Hyde syndrome, this guy can swing from furiously shouting to curled up in the fetal position sobbing in a matter of minutes. We've got one word for you: manipulation. He doesn't like the news, and instead of taking it like a man with perspective and keeping his dignity, he's trying the Hail Mary of emotional turmoil. Think about it. He's either trying to scare you into staying with him or hoping pity will couple you in eternal bliss. The reasons he's resorting to this reaction are probably the same root causes behind why he's not the guy for you. Politely say, "I'm sorry" and remove yourself from the situation.

Bait and Switch Warning: When a girl breaks up with a guy, the biggest problem is his pride. He has lost the game. So many times he will do everything in his power to get you back and let you know everything is perfect. Then he'll dump *you.* That way he feels he won the game. So watch out for the ol' switcheroo.

El Rejectador

Men, for the most part you are good guys. You want to be the hero, the guy girls dream of, and breaking up with them doesn't fit the profile. So it may seem easier to just stop calling as much. Start getting busier with school or work or whatever, and then you can just fade off into the distance. Let us just say that first, it doesn't work that way, and second, it lacks respect and responsibility. You have to be a man. Hey, you were man enough to get into the relationship, so be man enough to get out. Face-to-face. Suck it up, be honest, and do it.

But you need to understand this before you start: Girls are talkers. They think and process stuff verbally, out loud. *With emotion*. They talk in order to think stuff through; it's weird, we know, but it's the truth. So they are going to have to talk it out. They are going to have to get all the stuff, all the questions, all the confusion out. That's okay . . . to a point. Don't take any of it as a personal attack. Try watching *The Godfather* beforehand and repeat to yourself the quote "It's just (the rejection) business; it's nothing personal." And stuff marshmallows in your mouth.

Seriously, you've had lots of time to process the breakup. For her it's new news, a fresh wound that she's having to deal with. So don't attack back. Don't point the fault finger at her. Just listen to her and try to understand that she has to get this stuff out.

The Clean Break

The clean break is crucial. A breakup is never anything you can make better by talking more or by giving in. By its very nature it is going to be a huge change for both of you, so the best thing you can do is make a clean break. "But how do I do that?" we hear you shouting. All right,

A Rejection Story
by Michael

One of the toughest habits I had to break was trying to get the other person to reject me when I really didn't want them anymore. I was one of those guys who had twisted thoughts that it'd be easier to get a girl to not like me than to tell her I didn't want her in my life. It usually worked like the destructive charm that it was . . . usually. This upside-down exercise finally ended when I met someone who wouldn't end things no matter how bad it got. I basically turned into a Tasmanian devil of self-destruction—all because I didn't want to reject someone. What a genius.

calm down, here are some breakup buffet choices. All-you-can-eat rejection.

You can try the quick route or the longer route. Decide based on what you know about you and your soon-to-be ex and the ever-popular direct proportion to the length and intensity of the relationship rule. If you just can't bear to talk about it too much, then go for the short version. But if you know that they will really need some time to talk it through, then go for the long version. And also, check

Rejecting someone is like taking off a Band-Aid. Would you rather do it slow or fast?

out your common sense. If you haven't been going out that long, make it short and sweet. If you've invested a lot into the relationship, then you may need more time to get through it.

The Short Breakup (10–15 Minutes)

1. Get them alone (or relatively alone) somewhere where you can talk. Note: If you are afraid of the person, don't go somewhere where you will be alone. Go public and have some backup around somewhere close.
2. Be calm—no mean looks or nasty comments.

3. Keep eye contact while you are talking, but don't feel like you have to stare at them. Looking down can be a sign of respect, and that's okay. Don't stare at the floor the whole time, though. Look at them as need be.
4. Get right to the point. You are there to break up, not to talk about the last game or the project you have due next week.
5. Tell them you have really appreciated getting to know them, but things are changing for you and you don't feel like you used to.
6. Don't say, "I just want to be friends," or even, "We can still be friends." Don't give them any opening that might make them think they still have a chance.
7. Don't blame them for the breakup.
8. If they get mad, don't get mad back or feel hurt. It's just part of the process.
9. Don't talk too much. You don't have to explain the reasons you want to break up. All they need to know is that you don't feel like dating them anymore, and that is your choice. If they ask you questions about why, you don't have to say anything except that you just don't feel the same way anymore. You don't have to give them every feeling you've had throughout

the process of coming to this decision. That's your private world, and telling them will only make them feel worse.

10. Don't let them change your mind. This is the first they have heard of the breakup, even though you've had time to process it, so they might do all they can to change your mind. If they push this, just tell them that this isn't a negotiation and you have to leave.

11. Don't be afraid of silence. You may say what's on your mind and receive dead silence in return. Do not fill the silence by talking and trying to explain more. Just power through. Let them break the silence if they want to.

A Rejection Story
by Hayley

I once—okay, maybe twice—let a guy talk me out of breaking up with him. By the time we were finished discussing why I just wasn't feeling it, he had convinced me I could change and learn to start feeling something. So the relationship dragged on into more and more agony for both of us. I take full responsibility for not sticking to my guns and instead being too afraid to hurt him.

1. Get them alone (or relatively alone) somewhere where you can talk. Note: If you are afraid of the person, don't go somewhere where you will be alone. Go public and have some backup around somewhere close.
2. Be calm—no mean looks or nasty comments.
3. Keep eye contact while you are talking, but don't feel like you have to stare at them. Looking down can be a sign of respect, and that's okay. Don't stare at the floor the whole time, though. Look at them as need be.
4. Get right to the point. You are there to break up, not to talk about the last game or the project you have due next week.
5. Tell them you have really appreciated getting to know them, but things are changing for you and you don't feel like you used to.
6. Now shut up and let them think about it. This is news to them, and they need time to process.
7. When they try to argue with you about breaking up, just listen and let them get it out.

8. After they've said what they needed to say, tell them you're sorry, but you just aren't going to change your mind.

9. Allow them to try another angle. But repeat that you're sorry, but you've made your decision.

10. If your relationship is complicated (you work together, carpool, play co-ed softball, etc.), define the new terms of the relationship. How will you interact in the future? You should have already figured this out before you got here. Be very clear. This isn't a vote. You are telling them how it will work. Always lean toward severing contact if at all possible.

11. They will want to talk and maybe argue with you about this too. Take the time to listen to them, but stick to your guns. You have a right to decide how you conduct your life.

12. It's normal for you to want to show emotion. You might not be able to avoid it, but don't be more emotional than the person you're rejecting. Nothing like upstaging the rejected!

13. Talk until they feel like they've talked it all out or for one hour, whichever comes first. There's no need to drag this on; it won't make their pain any better, and it will only make yours greater.

84

The biggest problem when breaking up is figuring out what to say. Here are some ideas. Again, this doesn't cover everything. If these don't work for you, figure out something different. These statements are clear, and they lay the responsibility on you. This is very important. They also make it clear that it is your choice and not theirs. Your soon-to-be ex needs to know that they can't argue with you about it because it's a decision you have already made. Don't water down your decision or give them an escape clause that will only drag out the relationship that you want to end.

Don't water down your decision or give them an escape clause that will only drag out the relationship that you want to end.

Some things to say when you want to break up with someone:

- "I've decided that I don't want to date you anymore."
- "I don't want to pursue this relationship anymore."
- "This relationship doesn't feel right to me, so I have decided not to see you anymore."
- "I don't see a future between us, so I'm going to stop dating you."

Say something like one of these. It's short, it's easy, it's to the point. And there's no wiggle room. These statements don't leave any room for them to argue. After you say your piece, they might try to argue with you, but stand firm. All you have to do is emphasize the fact that you have already made your decision and the relationship is definitely ending. There is nothing for them to argue because you aren't changing your mind.

Maybe it will make more sense if you can compare this to some things *not* to say. Check it out.

What *Not* to Say . . .

- **"It's not you, it's me."** This might be true, but nobody *ever* believes it. It's human nature that when someone rejects you, you assume it's because of something you did. So this statement just sounds like a lie, even if it isn't. The important thing is that you've made a decision, and you have a right to decide what you do with your life. They can't argue with *your* decision about *your* life, so keep it to that.
- **"I don't think I want to see you anymore."** The statement "I don't think" is a weak one. It sounds like you aren't quite sure, and that gives the other person an angle. They'll get a glimpse of your uncertainty, and they will pounce. This will lead to a series of arguments where they will try to convince you that you should think differently. Don't go there—it only makes things messy.
- **"I don't feel the same for you as you feel for me."** How the other person feels about you isn't the issue, so don't bring it up. You can only talk about how *you* feel. You can't assume

It's human nature that when someone rejects you, you assume it's because of something you did.

you know anybody else's feelings. That's kind of arrogant. If you say this, they will want to argue with you to prove that they *don't* feel more than you or that you *do* feel more than you say. Way off topic. Don't give them something to argue about. You want to make a clean break.

- **"I think we should just be friends."** *You can't just be friends.* The world has changed. You both liked each other, but now one of you doesn't. So that leaves one person still in like with one who is totally out of it. That spells trouble.

  The "let's be friends" thing is your selfish side talking, not your protective side. It seems like a good idea and all. It will make everything easier, and you get to keep the person in your life so you won't be totally lonely, right? But it's a lie! You may want this to happen, but it can't happen. Not right now, anyway. You have to have separation. If you don't, it's like you are trying to tear down a house and rebuild it at the same time. You have to totally destroy the old before you can rebuild the new.

  Plus, while going from boyfriend/girlfriend to friend removes the word *boy* or *girl*, you don't really think that you're removing their gender and all the emotions and times you've shared too, do you? Don't take the "boy" or the "girl" out of the person by making them your "friend." Leave them with their pride and their manhood/womanhood.

- **"I like somebody else more than you."** This is just downright cruel. They don't need to know this. It might make the breakup more obvious for them, but it will also make them feel cheated on, devalued, and lied to. You don't need to burn bridges when breaking up. This is a person, with feelings, and you are supposed to protect them. Don't rub their replacement in their face. Just tell them you don't want to date them anymore, and if they ask why, say, "I just don't see us together in the future." They can't argue with how you feel. If at all possible, stay away from talking about other people. But if they know you well enough and you are really close, they will probably know the truth. If they straight-up ask about you liking someone else, just say, "Yes, I do." If they don't ask, don't go into it. If they do, be short and honest. You don't have to explain.

- **"Can we take some time off?"** Chicken! Do you really want time off, or do you just want to get off easy? If it's the first, then you probably want time off so you can go out with other people. So just break up, already. If it's the second one, then we've got news for you: You aren't letting anybody off easy. You are only prolonging the pain. And the longer you let them hang onto hope, the more you're punishing them in the process, and the more it will hurt you down the

Only turkeys are chicken about rejection.

road. Rejecting someone honestly and cleanly is noble. But can you live life as the punisher? What seems like pain now will be nothing compared to what it will be like after they have hung on for weeks or months or even years in the no-man's-land of a relationship void. So just tell them now that you don't want to see them. Don't candy-coat it to save their feelings, because you aren't saving anything.

- **"Do you think we should keep dating?"** Wow, there's nothing like giving up your freedom of choice to someone else just because you aren't mature enough to say what you want. You may not be 100 percent sure, but don't ask the other person. Have your mind made up, and then tell the person that you want to break up. Don't put it onto them or play some kind of game.
- **"I don't want to date anyone right now."** Sure, this may be what you are thinking and feeling right now. But when you break up with this person and next week feel differently and start dating someone else, you become a liar. Don't rationalize this. Just understand that if you tell a person that you don't want to go out with them because you don't want to date anyone right now, then you'd better not jump into another relationship.
- **"God told me to break up with you."** Where in the Bible did he say that? The only time you know for sure that God has told you to get out of a relationship is when it's against his Word. Pretty basic. You'd better have video footage of the

burning bush if you pull this one. And please, for the love of
Pete and Patricia, don't use this especially, *especially* if the
person you are breaking up with is not a Christian. Don't let
that be your witness. Leave them with grace, not with a bad
taste about a God who told you to break their heart.

The Buck Stops Where?

You may think it's a lot easier to blame someone else than
to take responsibility yourself, but beware. You can really
get messed up if you start putting blame everywhere but on
you. Here are some ways you might blame someone else.

1. God wants me to spend more time with him. Stop.
   Don't go there. When you bring God into it like this,
   you blame him for what you are choosing to do and
   for your maturity level. If it is true that you aren't
   spending enough time with him, that is your fault,
   not God's or the other person's. People all over the
   world have amazing spiritual lives and are dating
   and even married. That is a cheap excuse for why
   you want to break up. So don't go there.
2. My friends/parents told me I had to break up with
   you. Don't use this excuse if it isn't true. Blaming

others is the coward's way out. Own up to your own decisions—if you don't do it now, you'll be a coward the rest of your life.

3. My work is just too important to me. So what happened? Wasn't work (or school) important before, when things were going well? The point here is to tell the truth. And blaming is never the real truth. You are breaking up because you don't want to date them anymore. If you did, nothing would get in your way. So be honest with them, and be honest with yourself. Don't play the blame game.

4. You just aren't who I thought you were. Ouch. There's no need to blame the other person for your decisions, even if they didn't measure up to your expectations. Keep that idea to yourself. Your job isn't to hurt the other person; it is to make the breakup as clean and painless as possible. So don't bring their shortcomings into it. It won't help anything.

Play the blame game and you'll end up looking like this.

Rejector's Checklist: Do's and Don'ts

Your Breakup "Do" List

You'll need to think about these things ahead of time:

- Give them the time they need to work through their feelings.
- Tell them a little about your relationship that was good.
- Tell them a little about them that you admire.
- Take responsibility for the breakup ("I'm just not ready for this relationship," "I'm moving and I can't keep up this relationship," etc.).
- Spell out the rules of separation (no more movies together, hanging out at each other's houses, carpooling, etc.).
- Be firm; don't leave an open door for them to sneak back in and change your mind.

93

Your Rejection "Don't-Do" List

- Don't offer to "just be friends," ever!
- Don't get critical and blame them for the breakup.
- Don't let them guilt you into changing your mind; their feelings are their responsibility, not yours.
- No hitting below the belt—"you're just not attractive enough," "your breath stinks," etc.
- Don't worry about being the bad guy (or girl); you have a right to your own choices.
- Don't expect it to go easy. Be prepared for them to fight your decision, but stand your ground.

Your Rejection Escape Route

If they handle the breakup badly, remember that their emotions aren't in your control. You should do what you can to be kind and gentle, but how they react is their responsibility. Everyone has to handle their own emotions. If they start weirding out on you, just tell them that their actions are making you uncomfortable and the conversation is over. We know it sounds harsh, but now is not the time to be Dr. Phil. It's time to figure out how to get out of there.

The Nuclear Option—A Broken Engagement

No one wants to get this far down the road and deal with rejection, but how do you deal with breaking things off when you're engaged? Well, wouldn't you know it, we've lived through those scenarios too!

Right now, you need to put out of your mind any thoughts about gifts, security deposits, invitations, reservations, and the like. Those aren't germane (or Tito) to the subject at hand, but we'll give you advice on those little details in a sec.

The first thing to do is revisit the little things/deal breakers concept to help you understand if this is just normal marriage jitters or necessitates deployment of the weapon of mass rejection. Once again, here are some examples of what could fall into these categories:

Little Things:
- body odor
- sound of their laugh
- eating habits
- nervous ticks
- their relationship with their mother
- Diet Coke over Diet Pepsi

Deal Breakers:

- wanting kids versus not wanting kids
- where they want to ultimately live
- lifestyle and financial status
- faith
- lack of chemistry
- no evidence of love—includes things like abuse, lies, and destructiveness

Some relationships just don't add up.

Essentially, you're having normal marriage jitters if you're obsessing about any of the little things. Now, if you're listing an endless string of little things, something is up. And when you get into the deal breakers of faith, family, finances, and evidence of love, you may have grounds for calling things off.

If your soon-to-be spouse doesn't want kids, doesn't share your faith, has a totally different view of debt and money management, or just doesn't seem to love you anymore (or to be someone you love), these are legitimate grounds for breaking things off.

Hopefully you're discovering these differences during or shortly after premarital counseling. If not, you've got to put the brakes on **now** to keep from feeling railroaded into a marriage you don't want. Regardless of the timing, seek wise counsel that has nothing invested in the event itself. In other words, if your family or in-laws are using the event to stage a long-awaited family reunion, you might seek advice from someone else first. You don't need to hear "What about all those plane tickets?!" when you first broach the topic.

Rejection Threat Level Green, Yellow, or Red?

We're not premarital counselors, but from our experience, you really only have three choices. You can:

1. Go through with it
2. Put things on hold
3. Break things off completely

Number one sometimes seems like the easiest option, but it can lead to marital ruin later in life. In dealing with number three, you'll need to put to use all of the rejection wisdom in this book and then some. Number two can be your problem child. Here's why. Most weddings are deposit- and date-driven. When you're having doubts, it's like a deafening doomsday clock that everyone tells you can't be stopped from ticking. Check out this list of inexcusable excuses for why you can't slow things down:

"The invitations have been sent."

"Family's travel is already booked."

"Deposits are non-refundable."

"The church or reception hall we want isn't available any other time."

"My parents will kill me."

These so-called reasons to go through with it pale in comparison to marrying someone you have serious doubts about being able to stay committed to because of deal break- ers. Listen, plans can be cancelled, money can be replaced, other buildings can be rented, and your parents will get over it. Absent the little things, the biggest deal breaker is that you're not sure you can keep the commitment to be with this person forever.

When we got married to each other, we both had pre- wedding jitters. We wondered about some little things, but we never doubted the essentials like faith, family, chemistry, and evidence of love. Even with a couple of pessimistic voices outside our trusted circle, the absence of any deal breakers drowned their voices out and brushed aside the little things as just that—little things.

If you decide to try to slow things down, just remember that in a way, you're temporarily rejecting the other person. No matter how cool they seem about it, they're going to feel like they're not good enough, and that might do enough damage to end the relationship. We're not trying to scare you off from option two, slowing down, but we don't want you surprised if they give you an ultimatum: "Either you want to marry me or you don't!"

The rule on ultimatums: the answer is always *no*. You don't want to live with someone who learns they can get what they want in spite of your feelings just by issuing an ultimatum. Bad news.

Roger Rejector says, "Just say NO" to ultimatums.

If you're staring straight in the face of a deal breaker and plans have been made, the dress has been bought, and the cake has been baked and frosted, we feel your pain. Remember, rejecting someone over deal breakers before marriage always brings "better" for both of you. If you're like we were and are feeling some jitters over little things, welcome to the club, and best wishes walking down the aisle. Marriage is well worth it.

Cleaning Up

4

Can We Still Be Friends?
(And Other Rejection Questions That Need Answers)

Can we still be friends after we break up?

No. Sorry. We know that's not what you want to hear, and yes, we see you stomping up and down with clinched fists, screaming "Yes we can, yes we can!" And we're sad. Sad for you, because one day you will see that it just doesn't work. The trouble, our dear sassy reader, is that when you break up, generally one person does the breaking. That means one person is being broken. And because of this messed-up situation, one person generally feels hurt by the other, and that doesn't just disappear and become a loving friendship. Trying to be "just friends" is the biggest lie we tell each other. The one saying it doesn't mean it, and the one hearing it really wants to be more than friends! Take our advice and don't ever say, "Let's just be friends." It won't work.

also see "The Prostitution of Being 'Just Friends'" on page 40.

Do I have to say "I want to break up," or can I just stop calling and avoid the person?

We can't believe you are even asking this one. Do you have to tell the person you've made a bond with that the bond is breaking? Hmmm . . . uh . . . *yes!* You **have** to. There is no way to live up to your full potential as a person of character other than to care about other people's feelings even when that might be hard on you.

Can I call the person who broke up with me just to talk?

When you get dumped, you so badly want to find out the real reason behind it, and that's why calling to "just talk" isn't the whole truth. You wanna know, was it something you did, or said, or didn't do? What's "your" problem? Well, life isn't all about you, and it's not all about you understanding. See, if you really cared about the other person, then you could let them make their own decision and leave them alone. They decided to stop seeing you, so you really have no right to invade their life with all your questions meant only to make you feel better. And you know what else? When you call them, it only makes them dislike you more. It makes them uncomfortable, and they now associate that uncomfortable feeling with you, because you are the reason they feel it. The best thing you can do when you've been dumped is to say good-bye and never call them to whine, complain, or try to fix things. That is a position of weakness and is very unflattering and selfish. Plus, have you not realized after reading this book that rejection set you free? So don't call "just to talk." It makes things messy, and in the end you just leave them disliking you even more.

Why did they tell me they loved me and then break up with me?

This happens a lot. And it's because they probably felt something at the time, but it might have been indigestion. But the more you study and experience love, the more you realize that love isn't a feeling, it's an action. But this isn't a book about love; it's about rejection, so we'll save this discussion for another time. Don't blame them and get all bitter about them not loving you right. This only pollutes your spirit. Accept the fact that you are going to reject or be rejected by everyone except your future spouse.

Will I ever get over this pain?

Have you ever bent your fingernail completely backwards so that it almost pulls off your skin? Or have you ever been hit in the nose or any other sensitive part of your body? Do you remember how it hurts for a long time? Well, that's the way rejection can feel. But when you take a blow to the body, do you ever come out better for it? Rarely. But with rejection, you're actually getting out of a situation that isn't good. And you're freed up to find one better. Somewhere along the way, you lost perspective. You made your relationship your idol. You filled in the blanks on the marriage certificate in your mind a tad premature. The sooner you gain the proper perspective, the sooner the pain will melt away. Try to remember that.

Aren't I good enough for them?

Yes, you are good enough, but you aren't *for* them. These are two different issues. Your goodness has nothing to do with them. You are two different people with two different lives that happened to cross. Just because this person has rejected you as their love doesn't mean you are defective or bad.

> What if my ex is now starting to call me to do things together? Does that mean they like me again? What do I do?

Crackers! This one is tough. There are two possibilities here, and it will be up to you to figure out which one applies to your situation.

One is that they were just scared when they broke up with you—too much pressure and all, so they let some pressure off with the breakup. Now they are feeling not so trapped, so they give you a call to see if you are mad or resentful. If you act hurt, they will see that there is no hope and will disappear again soon. If you act nice and friendly but not overly friendly, they might start to think, "Hmm, maybe they aren't too clingy and I was just freakin' for no reason. I kinda miss 'em." That's one option.

A Rejection Story
by Michael

This is going to sound weird, but I felt so great when I finally rejected someone the right way. But at the same time, it was one of the hardest breakups I'd ever done. Maybe because my newly learned art was bucking around twenty years of muscle memory. Maybe because there was really nothing wrong with her and this time it really was me. I remember at the time mourning the loss of the friendship but having a clear head about things because for once I had left no open door and made no excuses. I knew that better things were in front of me and by default were for her as well. The sooner you embrace this art, the sooner you'll be starting and ending relationships with grace until you find "the one." I only hope you start sooner than I did.

Cleaning Up

The second is that they are just lonely and know that you are a willing, easy catch. You loved them so much, so of course you'll come back—that is, until some other little hottie comes along to fill the void. Ouch! You don't want that. But the same thing still goes—no reason to get all huffy on the phone. They are not responsible for your emotions, so don't blame them. Be nice and friendly, but find out what is really going on. Why are they calling? What's going on in their life? How are things going? Have they been dating? You are going to have to play detective. And know this: If they have done this one before, run. It is just another round of heartache for you. There's no reason to start up something that will just end in major pain all over again.

We wish we could give you the magic words that let you know what your ex is thinking, but then that wouldn't be life. Life is a matter of learning things by falling down and getting back up again. Life is about inventing 9,000 ways not to make a lightbulb. You win some, you lose some, but you never stop running the race and going after the big prize. So watch, listen, and pray. Make an informed decision and stick with it!

Wasting time
deploring the past
keeps God at a
distance.

—Brennan Manning

The Lie of Partial Rejection

You need to keep in mind one more overarching concept on your rejecting journey. If you really want this thing you two have to be over, ingest this fact:

There is no such thing as partial rejection.

It's true, at least in the minds of those who don't appreciate the Art of Rejection. Because of the lack of perspective most of us have in regards to rejection, when someone tells us they "don't like us *that way*," we generally interpret it as "they don't like us *any way*." And when someone reacts to rejection like their whole world is imploding on them, as a compassionate human being who still has feelings for them, you are going to feel pulled to cave or compromise in the heat of the moment. You're going to feel pulled to water down your rejecting. Don't. Always keep in mind these two most important principles of rejection:

1. Any reason is a good enough reason.
2. There is no such thing as partial rejection.

Better Times Ahead

Whether you're the one doing the rejecting or the one being rejected, now that it's over, you are left with two options. You can *hang on* or *let go*.

No one can do this for you. No one can ease your pain. It's up to you. If you want to become the person God wants you to be, then you will look at this experience as another step on the path to the top of the mountain. It will be the only way that you can get from the dark valley to the top of the towering heights to bask in the sun. If you choose to get off this path of pain and head back down into darkness, you have no one to blame but yourself. But if you are a brave soul and choose to fight, to climb inch by inch up the rough terrain of pain, then we guarantee you that this experience with rejection will make your life better.

A wise soul sees that rejection is just another door eliminated in the process of finding the one we're looking for. He doesn't run and hide or return to the door to try the lock one more time. The wise soul fears nothing the world or others can throw at her. She has a healthy perspective that dating, like life, is fraught with rejection. And rejection is life's process of elimination for discovering your purpose.

A wise soul sees that
rejection is just another
door eliminated in the
process of finding the one
we're looking for.

Dealing with rejection when you've always thought it could only be a horrific thing is quite the life adjustment. But you can do it. Don't give up on love when you are going through this. It takes lots of falling down before you can learn to walk. And it can take lots of lost love to find your one true love. Just look at it like this: A breakup isn't a sign that you will be alone forever; it's just a sign that you are one step closer to finding "the one."

So take your life into your hands and commit to the process. This is your refining fire; this is the stuff that will make you into who you were meant to be. If you run from rejection, no work will be done in you, but if you learn to appreciate the Art of Rejection, you will see a better life with more and more possibilities. And not just in love. Whether you've found a precious find or rejection tells you it's merely fools gold, you'll actually start taking more risks and living in anticipation of something better down the road.

Edison practiced receiving rejection as an art form. And because of his perspective and perseverance, the whole world can turn on their bedside lamp to read this book without lighting a match. As for turning on the lamp on the other side of the bed, Edison left that invention up to you. Surely you can endure a few rejections short of 9,000 for love. In the meantime, there's always the Clapper.

Hayley DiMarco writes cutting-edge and bestselling books including *Mean Girls*, *Mean Girls All Grown Up*, *Sexy Girls*, *Technical Virgin*, *Marriable*, and *Dateable*. Her goal is to give practical answers for life's problems and to encourage readers to form stronger spiritual lives. Hayley is Chief Creative Officer and founder of Hungry Planet, an independent publishing imprint and communications company that feeds the world's appetite for truth. Hungry Planet helps organizations understand and reach the multitasking mindset, while Hungry Planet books tackle life's everyday issues with a distinctly modern spiritual voice.

Michael DiMarco has worked in publisher relations, coached volleyball at the university level, and co-hosted a relationship humor radio show called *Babble of the Sexes*. He is the CEO and Publisher of Hungry Planet, working with authors who wish to reach an increasingly postmodern culture with premodern truth. Michael is the coauthor of *Marriable*, *The Art of the First Date*, and *The Art of Rejection* with his wife, Hayley, and they live in Nashville, Tennessee.

"Feeding the World's Appetite for Truth"

What makes Hungry Planet books different?

Every Hungry Planet book attacks the senses of the reader with a post-modern mind-set (both visually and mentally) in a way unlike most books in the marketplace. Attention to every detail from physical appearance (book size, titling, cover, and interior design) to message (content and author's voice) helps Hungry Planet books connect with the more "visual" reader in ways that ordinary books can't.

With writing and packaging content for the young adult and "hip adult" markets, Hungry Planet books combine cutting-edge design with felt-need topics, all the while injecting a much-needed spiritual voice.

Why are publishers so eager to work with Hungry Planet?

Because of the innovative success and profitable track record of HP projects from the best-selling *Dateable* and *Mean Girls* to the Gold Medallion-nominated *The Dirt on Sex* (part of HP's The Dirt series). Publishers also take notice of HP founder Hayley (Morgan) DiMarco's past success in creating big ideas like the "Biblezine" concept while she was brand manager for Thomas Nelson Publishers' teen book division.

How does Hungry Planet come up with such big ideas?

Hayley and HP general manager/husband Michael DiMarco tend to create their best ideas at mealtime, which in the DiMarco household is around five times a day. Once the big idea and scope of the topic are established, the couple decides either to write the content themselves or find an up-and-coming author with a passion for the topic. HP then partners with a publisher to create the book.

How do I find out more about Hungry Planet?

Use the Web, silly—www.hungryplanet.net

The Art of Rejection